SURF'S UP!

Other Books by Jim Toomey

Sherman's Lagoon: Ate That, What's Next?

Poodle: The Other White Meat

An Illustrated Guide to Shark Etiquette

Another Day in Paradise

Greetings from Sherman's Lagoon:
The 1992 to 1993 Sherman's Lagoon Collection

Treasury

Sherman's Lagoon 1991 to 2001:
Greatest Hits and Near Misses

SURF'S UP!

The Sixth SHERMAN'S LAGOON Collection

JIM TOOMEY

**Andrews McMeel
Publishing**

Kansas City

Sherman's Lagoon may be viewed on the Internet at:
www.shermanslagoon.com

To Madeleine

8

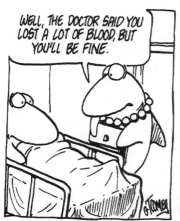

SHERMAN'S LAGOON

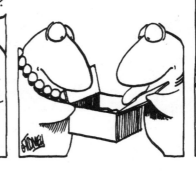

14

SHERMAN'S LAGOON

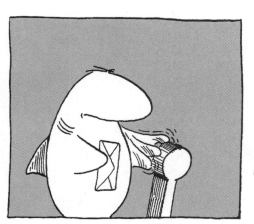

HE JUST OPENED HIS CREDIT CARD STATEMENT WHILE STANDING ON A SCALE.

HE'S CONFRONTING ALL HIS POST-HOLIDAY SHOCKS AT ONE TIME.

SHERMAN'S LAGOON

17

SHERMAN'S LAGOON

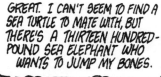

SHERMAN'S LAGOON

I ALWAYS GET A KICK OUT OF PLAYING THAT VIDEO BACKWARDS.

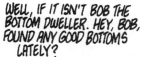

23

SHERMAN'S LAGOON

WHAT'RE YOU GOING TO WEAR TONIGHT, SHERMAN?

I DON'T KNOW. I HAVEN'T THOUGHT ABOUT IT.

DO YOU THINK THIS IS TOO MUCH?

MEGAN! MY GOODNESS! YOU KNOW HOW I FEEL ABOUT GIANT FRUIT-COVERED HATS!

NEEDS SOMETHING TO GO WITH IT.

WHADAYA THINK?

MEGAN! YOU'RE GOING ALL OUT!

NOW I NEED TO ACCESSORIZE A LITTLE... MAYBE THIS PURSE...

I SUPPOSE YOU'LL BE WANTING ME TO GET ALL DRESSED UP NOW, HUH?

I THINK THAT WOULD BE NICE.

OKAY... FINE... I'LL NEED SOME TIME TO PULL SOMETHING TOGETHER.

DUM DEE DAH DUM DUM ... LET'S SEE. NOPE... NOPE... MAYBE... HMMM HMMM HMMM... DUM DEE DUH DUM... HOW ABOUT THIS? PERFECT.

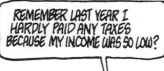

SHERMAN'S LAGOON

SHERMAN'S LAGOON

28

"YOUR PERMANENT LIFETIME ANSWER TO BALDNESS."

YOU SENT FILLMORE TO SOME HAIR TRANSPLANT DOCTOR WHO ADVERTISES IN PEOPLE MAGAZINE?

NO WORRIES, MEGAN, I'M SURE HE'S QUALIFIED.

IGOR...FETCH STYLING MOUSSE.
YES, MASTER.

FILLMORE?
WHAT DO YOU THINK OF MY NEW HAIR TRANSPLANT, SHERMAN?

WOW...THAT'S A LOT OF HAIR. WHERE'D THEY GET ALL THAT HAIR?
HUH?

WHO WAS THE DONOR?
GOT ME.

IT WASN'T A POODLE, WAS IT?
WHAT KIND OF A QUESTION IS THAT?

I GOT MY NEW DOO TRIMMED, SHERMAN, WHADDAYA THINK?

PRETTY COOL.
I HAD 'EM TAKE A LITTLE OFF THE SIDES...

STYLIN'
...AND THE BACK NEEDED MORE SHAPE, SO HE TRIMMED IT THERE.

I LIKE THE FLAT TOP. IT'S SORT OF THE M.C. HAMMER LOOK.
THAT WAS FROM AN OUTBOARD MOTOR.

Panel 1: HAWTHORNE, I'M WORRIED... EVER SINCE FILLMORE GOT THAT HAIR TRANSPLANT, HE'S BEEN ACTING VERY STRANGE.

Panel 2: I THINK THEY MIGHT HAVE USED DOG HAIR... I THINK IT MIGHT BE AFFECTING HIS BRAIN.

Panel 3:

Panel 4: YOUR TURN TO THROW THE TENNIS BALL. | OH, ALL RIGHT.

Panel 5: SNIFF SNIFF

Panel 6: HEY! KNOCK IT OFF!

Panel 7: HONESTLY, FILLMORE, EVER SINCE YOU GOT THAT HAIR TRANSPLANT, YOU'VE BEEN ACTING WEIRD... I THINK THEY USED DOG HAIR, AND NOW IT'S GOTTEN TO YOUR BRAIN!

Panel 8: WAS THAT THE CAN OPENER? | OOH! DINNER TIME!

Panel 9: FILLMORE, LISTEN. I'VE GOT SOME BAD NEWS... THAT HAIR TRANSPLANT YOU GOT... THEY USED POODLE HAIR ON YOU.

Panel 10: IT'S AFFECTING YOUR BRAIN, FILLMORE... YOU'RE SLOWLY BECOMING A POODLE. | I AM?

Panel 11: I'M TRYING TO SEE BEYOND THIS POODLE EXTERIOR OF YOURS, BUT IT'S HARD. | I'M STILL YOUR BEST BUDDY, SHERMAN, REMEMBER THAT.

Panel 12: OFF THE COUCH. | SORRY.

UH OH, I THINK FILLMORE WANDERED UP ONTO DRY LAND.

HAWTHORNE, THIS IS A DISASTER! SOCIETY WON'T KNOW WHAT TO MAKE OF HIM! HE'S A FREAK!... A MONSTROSITY!

WHO KNOWS WHERE HE'LL END UP.

INSTITUTIONALIZED, MAYBE.

WORSE. GERALDO.

I'M A LITTLE WORRIED, HAWTHORNE. FILLMORE'S BEEN MISSING FOR TWO DAYS NOW. IT'S NOT LIKE HIM.

FILLMORE, IT'S YOU! WHERE ARE YOU?

I'M AT A PAY PHONE ON A BEACH SOMEWHERE...IT'S BIZARRE. THE GROUND'S SHAKING, THE HILLS ARE ON FIRE, PEOPLE ON ROLLERBLADES ARE SHOOTING AT EACH OTHER...

JUST SLOWLY BACK OUT OF THERE, AND DON'T MAKE ANY SUDDEN MOVES... I THINK YOU'VE WANDERED INTO CALIFORNIA.

WOW... I'M IN CALIFORNIA!... SWIMMING POOLS... MOVIE STARS...

ARNOLD SCHWARZENEGGER!

I'VE SEEN ALL OF YOUR FILMS, MR. SCHWARZENEGGER. I'M A BIG FAN, BIG FAN.

FORGIVE ME FOR SAYING THIS, BUT YOU LOOK BIGGER ON THE SCREEN.

YA, DAT'S SHOWBIZ, KID.

SHERMAN'S LAGOON

MEGAN? IS THAT YOU?

I'VE JOINED THE GUERRILLA GIRLS, SHERMAN.

THE WHAT?

IT'S A RADICAL FEMINIST GROUP.

I'M TIRED OF BEING TREATED LIKE A SEX OBJECT BY ALL THE MEN AROUND HERE... IT'S TIME TO FIGHT BACK.

IN A GORILLA OUTFIT?

DO YOU THINK IT MAKES ME LOOK FAT?

IF MEGAN CAN HAVE HER WOMEN'S CLUB, WHY CAN'T WE HAVE A MEN'S CLUB?

GREAT IDEA... WE CAN MEET ONCE A WEEK AND SPOUT BOMBASTIC PLATITUDES AT ONE ANOTHER.

PLASTIC BOMBATITUDES... I LIKE THE SOUND OF THAT.

WE NEED A NAME.

THE McLAUGHLIN GROUP.

IT'S TAKEN.

THE FIRST MEETING OF THE MEN'S MOVEMENT HAS NOW BEGUN. SHERMAN HAS ARRANGED THE ENTERTAINMENT... SHERMAN.

THIS IS POSSIBLY ARNOLD'S GREATEST FLICK. A REAL TOUR DE FORCE... "DIE SUCKER PART TWELVE."

QUESTION. WHY DO THEY CALL THIS A MOVEMENT?

DISCUSSION AFTER THE MOVIE.

SHERMAN'S LAGOON

Panel 1: SHERMAN, WHY ARE YOU WEARING AN APRON? YOU NEVER COOK. / I'M A NEW MAN, MEGAN.

Panel 2: I'VE CAST OFF MY MACHO EXTERIOR AND STARTED TO EXPLORE THE CULINARY ARTS.

Panel 3: THIS IS ONE OF THE ALL-TIME OVERLOOKED KITCHEN TOOLS, MEGAN... THE SQUEEGIE.

Panel 4: EXPLAIN. / IN CASE YOUR HOT DOG EXPLODES IN THE MICROWAVE.

Panel 5: YOU KNOW WHAT YOUR GENERATION NEEDS, ERNEST? A GOOD SLOGAN. / YEAH... LIKE "FLOWER POWER" OR "YOU CAN'T TRUST ANYONE OVER THIRTY."

Panel 6: HEY, I'VE GOT ONE... HOW ABOUT "YOU CAN'T TRUST ANYONE OVER THIRTY."

Panel 8: CUTE. / NOW GO PLAY WITH YOUR SKATEBOARD. / RIGHT.

Panel 9: ANY WAY YOU SLICE IT, KIDS, WHEN THE BABY BOOMERS RULED THE POP CHARTS, THE MUSIC WAS BETTER.

Panel 10: WHAT ABOUT THAT FOUR-YEAR FLIRTATION WITH DISCO?

Panel 12: DISCO... I DON'T RECALL DISCO. / HE'S IN A STATE OF DENIAL.

SHERMAN'S LAGOON

Panel 1: HAVE YOU EVER LOOKED AT A HOSTESS HOHO UP CLOSE? / SHERMAN, DON'T BOTHER ME NOW. I'M TAKING A TRIP DOWN MEMORY LANE.

Panel 2:  IF YOU UNROLL IT, YOU GET ABOUT 8 LINEAR INCHES OF HOHO. / REMEMBER THE SUMMER OF '67... THE SUMMER OF LOVE?

Panel 3:  WE WERE SO DIFFERENT THEN.

Panel 4:  I FEEL FOR THIS FLOWER... I AM THIS FLOWER... KUMBAYA. / HAVE YOU EVER LOOKED AT A TWINKIE UP CLOSE?

Panel 5:  WHAT KIND OF NAME IS "GENERATION X" ANYWAY?

Panel 6:  IT'S JUST FOR THE TIME BEING UNTIL YOU DEVELOP MORE OF A GENERATIONAL IDENTITY.

Panel 7:  BUT YOU BETTER WATCH OUT BECAUSE IF YOU LET PEOPLE CALL YOU THAT LONG ENOUGH, IT MIGHT STICK.

Panel 8:  RIGHT, LARD BUTT? / IT'S TRUE.

Panel 9:  I PUT THE WORD OUT ON THE INTERNET, FILLMORE.

Panel 10:  I'VE HEARD FROM THOUSANDS OF FELLOW MEMBERS OF SO-CALLED "GENERATION X."

Panel 11:  THE CONSENSUS IS THAT "X" IS A STUPID NAME FOR A GENERATION. FROM NOW ON, WE HAVE A NEW IDENTITY.

Panel 12:  THE PEPSI GENERATION? / WE'RE GOING FOR CORPORATE SPONSORSHIP.

HOW'S YOUR SEARCH FOR A NEW NAME FOR GENERATION X GOING, ERNEST?

I GOT A STRONG RESPONSE WHEN I PUT THE INQUIRY OUT ON THE INTERNET.

WE'VE COME UP WITH A NEW NAME FOR BABY BOOMERS TOO...

"THE EVIAN-SWILLING, BMW-DRIVING, STAIRMASTER MONKEYS."

CATCHY.

WHO THE HECK ARE YOU?

I'M THE HOOKAH-SMOKING CATERPILLAR... WANNA HIT?

NO, THANKS. WHY ARE YOU HERE?

BE WARNED — YOU'LL BE VISITED BY THREE GHOSTS TONIGHT. THEY'LL TAKE THE FORM OF THE BABY BOOMER PAST, PRESENT AND FUTURE.

HUMBUG! YOU'RE JUST A FIGMENT OF MY IMAGINATION! TAKE THAT SMELLY THING AND BE GONE.

I KNEW I SHOULDN'T HAVE GONE TO BED ON AN EMPTY STOMACH.

YOU'RE IN LUCK. I'VE GOT A PIZZA COMING.

I AM THE GHOST OF THE BABY BOOMER PAST.

LUCY IN THE SKY WITH DIAMONDS?

COME WITH ME, FILLMORE, I WANT TO SHOW YOU SOMETHING.

WHY, THAT'S ME! I'M A LITTLE KID!

GLUED TO A T.V. SET. YOU WERE INFATUATED WITH MRS. CLEAVER.

OH WELL, LOVE IS BLIND.

LOVE IS NEARSIGHTED. HORMONES ARE BLIND.

I AM THE GHOST OF THE BABY BOOMER PRESENT.

SONNY BONO?

MAYOR BONO... I WAS MAYOR OF PALM SPRINGS, YOU KNOW. WE'RE ALL GROWN UP. THERE'S EVEN A BOOMER IN THE WHITE HOUSE.

LOOK! THERE YOU ARE WATCHING "BEAVIS AND BUTT-HEAD," BUT YOU DON'T GET IT. YOU'RE NOT YOUNG AND HIP ANYMORE... NONE OF US ARE... EXCEPT FOR CHER.

HOW DOES SHE DO IT?

LIPOSUCTION.

I AM THE GHOST OF THE BABY BOOMER FUTURE.

DICK CLARK?

WOW... YOU HAVEN'T AGED A BIT.

FOLLOW ME, FILLMORE.

THERE'S YOUR FUTURE SELF... YOU'RE TELLING YOUR KIDS TO TURN THE RADIO DOWN.

C'MON, DICK, LISTEN TO THAT RACKET.

I REMEMBER THEY SAID THE SAME THING ABOUT MOZART.

WHEN WERE YOU BORN?

I'VE EMBRACED THE GRUNGE CULTURE, ERNEST.

HUH?

I'M CASTING OFF MY MATERIALISTIC YUPPIE WAYS.

I WANT TO BE A SLACKER AND THRASH ABOUT ON MY SKATEBOARD AND LISTEN TO PEARL JAM.

WOW... A DIGITAL SPEEDOMETER. WHERE'D YOU GET THE BOARD?

SHARPER IMAGE.

SHERMAN'S LAGOON

IT'S A SHIP FULL OF CANADIAN BACON! THIS IS THE THIRD NIGHT IN A ROW, MEGAN!

GO AHEAD, SHERMAN, HAVE YOUR BACON! THERE'S A WILDLY MYSTERIOUS MAN PERFORMING SPONTANEOUS ACTS OF ROMANCE ON ME AND, I MUST SAY, MY HEART'S AFLUTTER.

ZZZZ... MMM BABY.

MMM BACON.

SHERMAN'S LAGOON

SAYS HERE IN THIS MAGAZINE THAT SHARKS HAVE LITTLE OR NO MEMORY.

THAT'S THE MOST RIDICULOUS THING I'VE EVER READ.

WHAT IS?

THIS THING IN HERE.

NO PEEKING.

UH-OH, SHERMAN, LOOK. THEY'RE HAVING A CONTEST TO SEE WHO CAN HARPOON THE HEAVIEST SHARK IN THE LAGOON.

WHADAYA MEAN, "UH-OH, SHERMAN"?

WELL, YOU'RE THE BIGGEST LOAD WEIGHT IN THE LAGOON.

YOU'RE NO SPRIG OF WILD LAVENDER YOURSELF, MEGAN. HAVE YOU CHECKED YOUR WEIGHT LATELY?

I CHECK IT ALL THE TIME. IT NEVER CHANGES.

YEAH? PROVE IT.

LOOK. IT'S RIGHT HERE ON MY DRIVER'S LICENSE.

I'LL NEED TWO FORMS OF I.D.

THERE GOES THE FIRST LURE OF THE FISHING TOURNAMENT, MEGAN.

LET'S SEE IF IT GETS ANYBODY'S ATTENTION.

UH OH, CARL'S INTERESTED.

GO FOR IT, CARL!

WHOSE SIDE ARE YOU ON?

JUST TRYING TO LIVEN THINGS UP, MEGAN.

48

SHERMAN'S LAGOON

"LIFT UP YOUR HEARTS EACH NEW HOUR HOLDS NEW CHANCES FOR A NEW BEGINNING..."

"DO NOT BE WEDDED FOREVER TO FEAR, YOKED ETERNALLY TO BRUTISHNESS..."

THAT WAS WONDERFUL, SHERMAN.

MAYA ANGELOU IS MY FAVORITE POET. IT WAS SWEET OF YOU TO MEMORIZE SOME OF HER WORK.

WHATEVER MAKES YOU HAPPY, MEGAN.

DID YOU LEARN THAT STUFF I GAVE YOU?

UH... SORT OF. WANT ME TO RECITE IT?

THAT WOULD BE NICE.

AHEM

THE INFIELD FLY RULE.

LOUDER.

50

53

SHERMAN, I'M TIRED OF LIVING UP TO SOME SOCIETAL NOTION OF WOMANHOOD.

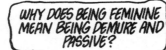
WHY DOES BEING FEMININE MEAN BEING DEMURE AND PASSIVE?

I SAY BALONEY. IT'S TIME WE WOMEN REDEFINED "FEMININE" ON OUR OWN TERMS.

LOOK. I GOT A TATTOO.

"NO FAT DUDES."

WHAT ARE YOU DOING, MEGAN?

I'M ADMIRING MY BICEPS IN THE MIRROR.

UH-UH. I'M GOING TO HAVE TO CALL YOU ON THAT ONE. THAT'S STRICTLY A GUY THING. GIRLS DON'T DO THAT.

THERE'S SOME KIND OF WEIRD GENDER REVERSAL GOING ON IN OUR RELATIONSHIP, AND I DON'T LIKE IT, MEGAN.

NOW, IF YOU'LL EXCUSE ME, I NEED TO CHECK MY EYE SHADOW.

BE MY GUEST.

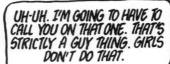

I'M GONNA HIT THE HEAD. BACK IN A SEC, GUYS.

I'M WORRIED ABOUT SHERMAN. HE AND MEGAN HAVE BEEN TOGETHER SO LONG THEY'RE STARTING TO ACT LIKE EACH OTHER.

BIG DEAL. COUPLES DO THAT.

BUT, HAWTHORNE, IT IS A BIG DEAL.

WHADAYA MEAN?

HE JUST WALKED INTO THE LADIES' ROOM.

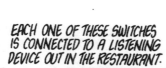

Panel 1: SHERMAN, WHERE HAVE YOU BEEN? / THE LADIES' ROOM.

Panel 2: HUH? / I ACCIDENTALLY WALKED INTO THE LADIES' ROOM... WOW... YOU GUYS WON'T BELIEVE IT.

Panel 3: I ALWAYS THOUGHT THEY WERE JUST LIKE MEN'S ROOMS. UH-UH. THEY HAVE A JACUZZI AND A MASSEUSE... ANTIQUES... PERSIAN RUGS...

Panel 4: THEIR TOILET PAPER IS MOUNTED TO THE WALL. / WHY DIDN'T WE THINK OF THAT?

Panel 5: KNOW ANY BEDTIME STORIES, SHERM? / A BEDTIME STORY, HUH? LET'S SEE...

Panel 6: ONCE UPON A TIME, GOLDILOCKS CAME HOME AND FOUND THREE BEARS IN HER HOUSE... AND THREE PIGS... AND A WOLF IN DRAG... AND A DUCK... A REALLY UGLY DUCK.

Panel 8: I GUESS YOU CAN TAKE THIS STORY ANYWHERE YOU WANT. / I'M THINKING.

Panel 9: BEN'S RETIRING. / BEN? OF BEN AND JERRY'S ICE CREAM? HE'S CALLING IT QUITS?

Panel 10: YEP. / BEN'S QUITTING... WOW. IT'S A DARK DAY FOR ICE CREAM, FILLMORE.

Panel 11: YOU KNOW, SOMETIMES I THINK I OWE MY EXISTENCE TO BEN AND JERRY'S ICE CREAM... OR AT LEAST PART OF IT.

Panel 12: 'BOUT 60 POUNDS OF IT, I'D SAY. / OH, GIVE OR TAKE.

SHERMAN'S LAGOON

LOOK, FILLMORE! A MASSIVE SCHOOL OF SHRIMP HEADED THIS WAY... MEDIUMS AND JUMBOS, AND THEY'RE LOOKIN' FOR TROUBLE.

I SAY WE DO A PRE-EMPTIVE STRIKE! LET'S GO! CHARGE!

FORGOT THE COCKTAIL SAUCE.

RIGHT HERE.

HA! FILLMORE! CHECK THIS OUT... A TREASURE CHEST.

WHAT A CLICHÉ... I DIDN'T THINK THOSE THINGS REALLY EXISTED.

LET'S SEE IF THERE'S ANYTHING IN HERE WORTH KEEPING.

PIECES OF EIGHT, GOLD DUBLOONS, TWO FRONT-ROW TICKETS TO A ROLLING STONES CONCERT, A DIAMOND TIARA.

WHOA, GO BACK ONE.

TWO FRONT-ROW TICKETS TO THE STONES CONCERT... WHO'RE YOU GONNA TAKE? WHO'S YOUR PAL, HUH?

FILLMORE, I DO BELIEVE YOU'RE GROVELING.

YES, BUT IT'S A CONTROLLED GROVEL, NOT A SHAMELESS GROVEL.

(SOB) I JUST REALLY WANNA GO TO THAT CONCERT... REALLY REALLY BAD... AWWWHAWW SHERMAN, PLEASE!

FILLMORE, I THINK YOU'VE VENTURED INTO SHAMELESS TERRITORY.

DID YOU NOTICE A TRANSITION?

SHERMAN'S LAGOON

65

66

SHERMAN'S LAGOON

SHERMAN'S LAGOON

YAHHOO!

I'M A FINALIST IN THE PUBLISHER'S CLEARINGHOUSE SWEEPSTAKES!

BIG DEAL. DID YOU GET ANY INTERESTING MAIL?

LET'S SEE... HMM... JUST FOR SHARKS... SPECIAL OFFER...

...FREE MOUTH WASH.

YAHH HOO!

ARE YOU IMPLYING THAT I HAVE BAD BREATH, HAWTHORNE?

YOUR BREATH IS LIKE FETID BILGEWATER FROM AN OLD TUNA TRAWLER.

THAT'S NOT A GOOD THING, IN CASE YOU WERE WONDERING.

I COULD TELL BY THE TONE OF HIS VOICE.

MEGAN, I WANT YOU TO BE FRANK WITH ME... DO I HAVE BAD BREATH?

THERE'S A CERTAIN SMELL TO IT, I GUESS.

SMELL? SMELL'S ONE OF THOSE WORDS THAT CAN GO BOTH WAYS. I WANT SPECIFICS.

THE KIND OF SMELL THAT WOULD KNOCK A BUZZARD OFF A MANURE TRUCK.

I WANT TO KNOW MORE ABOUT THIS BUZZARD.

BIG, BLACK BUZZARD.

SHERM, I'VE GOT A SOLUTION TO YOUR NASTY-SMELLING BREATH.

TWO WORDS: DENTAL HYGIENE... OPEN UP.

HMMM... DOESN'T LOOK TOO BAD... THE BACK TWO ROWS NEED SOME WORK.

DO YOU USE A TARTAR-CONTROL TOOTHPASTE WITH FLOURIDE?

MILK BONES.

HEY, HAWTHORNE, GOOD NEWS... NO MORE BAD BREATH... NOW IT'S FRESH AS A CAROLINA PINE FOREST... SMELL.

SNIFF

HMMMMMM...

ANY BEARS IN THAT PART OF THE COUNTRY?

YOUR POINT BEING?

LOOK! IT'S A HERD OF WHALES! THEY'RE GOING TO BEACH THEMSELVES!

A POD.

HUH?

THEY'RE CALLED "PODS."

REALLY?

SCOUT'S HONOR.

LOOK! IT'S A HERD OF PODS...

A POD OF WHALES.

THE EXXON PROZAC HAS RUN AGROUND AND SPILLED ITS CONTENTS INTO THE LAGOON!

LET'S SEE IF IT'S HAVING ANY EFFECT ON THE WHALES...

YES! THEY'RE TURNING AROUND! THEY'RE NOT GOING TO BEACH THEMSELVES AFTER ALL!

THEY'RE SAYING SOMETHING... LISTEN.

ERNEST, YOU UNDERSTAND WHALE... TRANSLATE.

I'M GOOD ENOUGH... I'M SMART ENOUGH... AND... DOGGONIT... PEOPLE LIKE ME...

MORNIN', SHERM.

MORNIN', ERNEST.

YOU KNOW, HAWTHORNE, EVER SINCE THAT SUPERTANKER SPILLED PROZAC INTO THE LAGOON, EVERYBODY'S BEEN SO HAPPY...

...YOU KNOW, PROZAC MAY PUT A SMILE ON YOUR FACE, BUT IT WON'T MAKE YOUR PROBLEMS GO AWAY.

AFTER ALL, YOU'RE STILL A PETTY, TOE-PINCHING CRUSTACEAN.

AND YOUR BREATH STILL SMELLS LIKE RAT VOMIT.

BEFORE PROZAC, MY LIFE WAS LIKE A CONTINUOUSLY LOOPING QUENTIN TARANTINO MOVIE... NOW IT'S "THE SOUND OF MUSIC!"

VRROOM!

SO LONG, FAREWELL, AUF WIEDERSEHEN, GOODBYE...

POP!

IT'S A LITTLE OF BOTH, I'D SAY.

SHOWOFF.

BOING!

79

HEY, SHERMAN, THAT BABY BOTTOMDWELLER OF YOURS HAS WANDERED OFF AGAIN.

WHAT? HEY! GET BACK HERE!

OKAY, YOU DON'T WANNA LISTEN? FINE.

WE'LL SEE WHO'S THE BIG FISH IN THIS POND.

HOLD MY BEER.

YOU'RE REALLY GETTING INTO THIS PARENTHOOD THING, AREN'T YOU?

NOTHING BUT THE BEST FOR MY BABY BOTTOMDWELLER.

I'M SHOWING HIM A POTTY TRAINING VIDEO. C'MON IN.

I DIDN'T KNOW THAT SEAT THING WENT UP AND DOWN.

LEARN SOMETHING NEW EVERY DAY.

FILLMORE, CAN YOU BABY-SIT MY BOTTOMDWELLER? I'VE GOT TO RUN OUT AND GET DIAPERS.

SURE. WHAT DO I DO?

JUST SIT HIM ON A FLAT SURFACE AND RUN THIS BARNEY VIDEO OVER AND OVER.

WHAT KIND OF SOCIETY IS THIS?

WHADDAYA SAY WE WATCH "MASTERPIECE THEATRE"?

PUT THE GUN DOWN.

WHAT ON EARTH ARE YOU DOING, SHERMAN? | **PARENTAL IMPRINTING. I'M TEACHING MY BABY BOTTOMDWELLER PROPER BOTTOM-DWELLING TECHNIQUES.**

FRANKLY, I THINK THIS PARENTAL IMPRINTING IS A CROCK. ALL HE DOES IS LOOK AT ME WITH THAT DUMB STARE. I GIVE UP.

TRY RAISING ONE ARM. | **YOU MEAN, LIKE THIS?**

WHAT'S THE MATTER, FILLMORE? | **I'M JUST A LITTLE WORKED UP ERNEST. THEY'RE HAPPY TEARS, THOUGH.**

YOU KNOW THAT LITTLE BOTTOMDWELLER SHERMAN ADOPTED? WELL, HE'S ALL GROWN UP NOW, AND HE'S READY TO FACE THE WORLD.

SHERMAN'S GIVING HIM A LITTLE FATHER-SON PEP TALK RIGHT NOW.

YOU'RE GOING STRAIGHT TO THE BOTTOM, KID.

TODAY'S THE BIG DAY, FILLMORE. TODAY MY PARENTING SKILLS GET PUT TO THE ACID TEST... IT'S TIME TO SET MY BOTTOMDWELLER FREE.

MAKE ME PROUD, LITTLE BOTTOMDWELLER.

HE CAN'T FIND THE BOTTOM. | **WHERE DID I GO WRONG?**

SHERMAN'S LAGOON

84

SHERMAN'S LAGOON

Panel 1: FILLMORE, YOU KNOW HOW I'VE ALWAYS INSISTED THAT ELVIS WAS KIDNAPPED BY ALIENS? — YEAH.

Panel 2: WELL, I WAS WRONG. HE'S BEEN DEAD ALL ALONG. — WELCOME BACK TO REALITY, SHERMAN.

Panel 3: HE'S REINCARNATED, AND HE'S LIVING RIGHT HERE IN THE LAGOON. — UH OH... WE'RE LOSING HIM AGAIN.

Panel 4: HE'S A CLAM. — JUST KEEP HUMORING HIM WHILE I GET THE TRANQUILIZER GUN.

Panel 5: FILLMORE, I SWEAR TO YOU I HEARD THIS CLAM SING, AND IT WAS THE VOICE OF ELVIS. ELVIS HAS RETURNED AS A CLAM.

Panel 6: HOW COULD THIS CLAM BE ELVIS? LOOK AT IT. IS THAT THE FACE OF THE KING?

Panel 7:

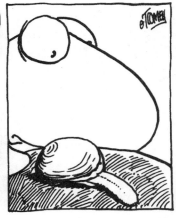

Panel 8: IT'S MICK JAGGER. — HE'S NOT DEAD.

Panel 9: SHERMAN, I THINK THIS REINCARNATION THEORY OF YOURS HAS SOME PLAUSIBILITY.

Panel 10: I MEAN, I, FOR ONE, AM CONVINCED I WAS A VIKING IN A PAST LIFE.

Panel 11: OH, COME ON, MEGAN... YOU? A VIKING? GET REAL.

Panel 12: HEE HEE HEE... MY LITTLE TULIP THINKS SHE WAS A VIKING. — THIS GUY'S HISTORY.

SHERMAN'S LAGOON

SHERMAN'S LAGOON

SHERMAN'S LAGOON

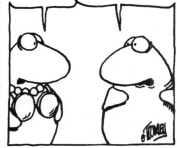

Panel 1: THIS IS ASCENCION ISLAND? THIS IS WHERE ALL THE SEA TURTLES COME TO MATE?

Panel 2: YEP.
WELL, THEY DON'T LOOK VERY EXCITED.

Panel 3: OH, THEY'RE EXCITED ALL RIGHT. ALMOST PASSIONATE, I'D SAY.
HOW CAN YOU TELL WHEN A SEA TURTLE HAS HIT THE PASSIONATE POINT?

Panel 4: WE PASS OUT.
NO WONDER YOU'RE ENDANGERED.

Panel 5: FILLMORE, THIS IS BORING. I THOUGHT THIS SEA TURTLE MATING EVENT MADE PLAYBOY MAGAZINE'S TOP TEN PARTY LIST.

Panel 6: I LIED. IT WAS ON NATIONAL GEOGRAPHIC'S TOP TEN PARTY LIST.
OH, FILLMORE.

Panel 7: WE WERE NUMBER TEN.

Panel 8: DUNG BEETLES WERE NUMBER NINE.
OH, FILLMORE.

Panel 9: WHADDAYA MEAN YOU'VE CHANGED BACK INTO A MAN?
THE DOCTOR SAID THIS GENDER TRANSFERENCE THING WAS TEMPORARY.

Panel 10: THIS CHANGES THE MATING STRATEGY A BIT.
I'D SAY.

Panel 11: YOU'RE NO LONGER A SINGLE GREEN FEMALE SEEKING A ROMANTIC INTERLUDE ON A MOONLIT BEACH.
NOW I'M A SINGLE GREEN MALE....

Panel 12: ...AND I'M MISSING THE BASKETBALL TOURNAMENT.
LET'S GO HOME.

SHERMAN'S LAGOON

100

SHERMAN'S LAGOON

SHERMAN'S LAGOON

SHERMAN... HAWTHORNE... GUYS... THIS MORBID FASCINATION WITH THE O.J. TRIAL HAS GONE TOO FAR... YOU'RE...

NEW TOY?

IT'S A JUDGE ITO ACTION DOLL.

YOU'RE ALL MORALLY BANKRUPT.

GUILTY!

HEY, HAWTHORNE, HOW'D YOU GET YOUR JUDGE ITO DOLL TO TALK?

JUST PULL HIS STRING, AND AWAY HE GOES.

ORDER IN THE COURT! ORDER IN THE COURT!

RATS. I CAN'T GET MY SHAPIRO DOLL TO TALK.

WAIT A SEC... WHAT'S IT SAY ON THE BACK THERE?

"FOR LEGAL ADVICE, INSERT FIFTY CENTS."

FRIGGIN' LAWYERS.

LOOK, HAWTHORNE, MY KATO KAELIN ACTION DOLL ARRIVED.

HE'LL BE A KEY WITNESS IN OUR MOCK O.J. TRIAL.

NEW KATO!

KATO RULES... HE'S SMARTER THAN EVERYONE THINKS, YA KNOW.

COOL! IT'S THE NEW CUT 'N' CURL KATO.

LOOK. YOU CAN MAKE HIS HAIR GROW.

I THINK SOMETHING'S WRONG WITH SHERMAN.

WOW. HE'S TOTALLY ZONED OUT.

YOU CAN MAKE FUNNY FACES, AND HE DOESN'T FLINCH.

SOMETHING'S UP.

YOU CAN EVEN BALANCE A TWINKIE ON HIS NOSE... NARY A BLINK.

INCREDIBLE.

AND WHEN DID SHERMAN EVER LET YOU FILL HIS NOSTRILS WITH CHEEZ WHIZ?

HARDLY EVER.

SHERMAN'S GONE CATATONIC. TOO MUCH O.J.

ANOTHER VICTIM OF THE SHAMELESS EXPLOITATION OF THIS TRAGIC EVENT.

LOOK AT US... WE'RE A CULTURE OBSESSED WITH VIOLENCE AND PROFIT. WE'VE ALL OVERDOSED ON O.J.

O.D.'D ON O.J. HMMM...

MAKE A PRETTY GOOD TEE SHIRT.

IT'S IRREVERSIBLE... HE'S BRAIN DEAD.

AND IT WAS THE MINDLESS REPETITION OF WATCHING THE O.J. TRIAL 8 HOURS A DAY THAT DID IT.

I THINK THE ONLY HUMANE THING TO DO IS TO FIND A PAINLESS WAY TO PUT HIM DOWN.

PULL THE PLUG? HOW?

STICK HIM IN A ROOM, PUT A 'BARNEY' VIDEO ON, AND LET HIM QUIETLY SLIP AWAY.

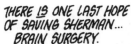
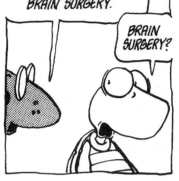

109

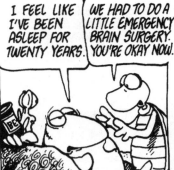

110

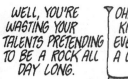

118

SHERMAN'S LAGOON

SHERMAN'S LAGOON

SHERMAN'S LAGOON

SHERMAN'S LAGOON